Common and Uncommon Thoughts

Poems about Thoughts of Being and Seeing

Hollis Davis

Path Publishing
Amarillo, Texas

First edition
Copyright © 2018 Hollis Davis

All rights reserved. This book or portions thereof may not be reproduced in any form without written permission from the publisher or the author except for brief passages used in reviews.

Path Publishing
4302 SW 51st #121
Amarillo, Texas 79109-6159
USA
Path@PathPublishing.com
PathPublishing.com

Cover photograph by Cristine Davis

To order copies, see About Path Publishing at the end of the book.

ISBN-13: 978-1-891774-70-6
ISBN-10: 1-891774-70-0

Printed in the United States of America

"I think, therefore I am."
Rene Descartes

Contents

Acknowledgments vi

Introduction 1

I. Thoughts and Sights 2

Common Thoughts 3
Found 4
How I See People, Things, and Ideas 5
Extra Day 6
Dreams 8
About the Past 9
Observation 10
Conscience or Science 11
Born to Surprises 12
Who Am I (Thinking) 14
Nature 15
Seeing things differently 16
Impossible 18
Why 20
American Indians 21

II. Love or Something Like It 22

Dried Dreams 23
A Pair 24
Beauty or Fashion 25
A New Day 26

Natural Art 28
Pretty 29
Words 30
Waking 31
Buttons 32
A Part of Me 33
Message Mistakes 34
A Selfie 36
Curds and Whey 38

III. Happenings and Descriptions 39

Fliver 40
Haikus for May 2017 41
Farmer, Ship Builder and Soldier 42
Getting By 43
Impact 44
Current events 45
Happenings 46
Animal Companions 48
Attached Light 50
The Sisyphean Game 51
Jungle Animal 52

About the Poet 53

About Path Publishing 54

Acknowledgements

These are new poems, some prepared for reading at The Tarrant County Poet Society. Two were read at a Poet Society of Texas meeting. The selections for this book were assisted by Lynn Lewis and Elaine Mango. They also did some editing for which I am thankful.

Thoughts are difficult to picture unless with balloons or circles above someone's head; therefore, it was difficult to select a cover for this book. But three on a boat watching a wading fisherman, with my son, Barry, trying to land a salmon, indicates that four people had a common thought. Maybe even five, since daughter-in-law Cristine took the picture.

We had several photographs to choose from, and the selection was made in a brainstorm session with Pansy, my wife, and Dan and Barbara Wall. My sons, Bruce and Barry, also had some input.

Introduction to Common and Uncommon Thoughts

This book of poems has been separated into three sections:

I. Thoughts and Sights
II. Love or Something Like It
III. Happenings and Descriptions

This book represents more of my mature thoughts, but many still seem immature. Maybe they are immature and I am still working on maturity in my writing and in my common and uncommon thoughts. My thoughts remind me of the Roger Miller song "Where Have All the Average People Gone?" The theme of the song is "How come I don't fit?" That may be an extreme thought, but some of my poems reflect that theme.

I believe that everyone will find a poem which will address their thoughts and maybe even some of their own reflections. Enjoy.

I. Thoughts and Sights

As readers and writers, we may be both right and wrong about certain points. Our experiences drive the arc of our individual stories, always crowd common and individually uncommon thoughts to show our differences.

Thoughts are some of what we are. We interpret our experiences differently. Reactions to sights are some of what makes us different from others when we are looking at the same sight. If we are close, we will see it at the same time but likely see it differently. If we are separated by even a small distance, we will even see the sight at different times.

Many of my thoughts are questions about things I do not understand. Sights also present questions about their creation and complexity. DNA has made some beautiful shapes of living things. The aging of the Earth has made some beautiful landscapes. This living on Earth and the views make our lives enjoyable.

Common Thoughts

My thoughts and words are common
Just as my stories that I often tell
When words become a famine
Common cognition is what I sell
There are words I could look up
In the thesaurus or the dictionary
But while drinking from the cup
I shall use my limited vocabulary
And feed off my cognitive muse
The most common of creation
Seems to be the words I choose
For my poetry communication
So this book of poems will be
Like all the rest I have written
Some common thoughts to see
The creation bug has bitten
It is me with cognition once again
Showing my happiness and my pain

Found

The most important thing I have found
Is that baby bluebirds have large mouths
When they are still nest-bound
Other things I have found
About our world I do not know
How trees, plants and veggies grow
How the Earth and sun are round
Seasons for growing come and go
Because the Earth is tilted so
Maybe that is all l need to know
I have found other mysteries that baffle me
Like when ideologies get too adverse
Citizens become isolated and transverse
I have found deeds I cannot comprehend
Observing man's behavior bad and good
Processes, I have not yet understood
But I can appreciate every day
As the morning light is unfurled
I see the beauty in this old world
I have found contours and designs
And an appreciation for the divine

How I See People, Things and Ideas

My past affects how I see what I see
So it is different for you and me
It is going to be difficult to know
Whether I should stay or I should go
The past has left some different imprints
That may even obscure what we sense
Even a change of color and size of what we see

And the importance of each for you and me
Some happenings may be out of place
There will be some we cannot erase
That will drive what we see askew
Leave us boggled without a clue
If we are to learn from our past
We must break the memory cast
Seems we must reassess ourselves
Take some memories off the shelves
Get rid of bias formed by the past
Not respond to the recent quite so fast
Adjust to what we see and hear
And what we have learned to fear

Extra Day

As the Earth moves rather slow
Eleven billion years on the go
It still can't get around on time
Every four years it's a day behind
It is named a day of leap
And it's a day we have to keep
It has added 21 days to my life
Along with 15 days with my wife
My extra age gets no recognition
Not even a bit of consideration
For those 21 extra days
I should receive a gift or praise
Appears that extra day is not for me
But for women to change destiny
It is a day for the female quest
Yet I have not received one request
And the time is getting late
Another marriage is not my fate
I may have another extra day
If I'll last I still can't say
The Earth may never catch up

I'll wait again for the interrupt
When in year 2020 I can say
I have added an extra day

Dreams

Why do I dream
Not of you
But
Where I used to work

Of workmates no longer alive

Searching for my car

Traversing over hill and dale

Searching for an office chair

Feeling left out

Having no constructive work

Looking for my hotel, motel room

Attending a conference

Being with employees from other companies

Searching for a bathroom

Why can't I just dream of you
Maybe I do

Maybe I will
I have some hope
Still

About the Past

Growing up on the farm is a memory most
people don't have anymore
Therefore for me to have a conversation about
pigs is a chore
Hog killing is no longer a community project in
the fall
When neighborhood camaraderie was the best of
all
It might include the neighbor musicians playing
a two-step fast
Even dancing with your neighbor's wife is a
thing of the past
Canning and subsistence farming held back the
poverty line
We didn't always know it but life on the farm
was just fine

Observation

She was

Sitting beside an older man

Staring at the window, uncomfortable

She did not want to be there

Two other ladies were there relaxed

She pushed her hair back behind her neck

She was apprehensive as she ate her salad

Seemingly awkward

Would she ever fit into this group

Conscience or Science

Was it conscience
Or was it science

That caused us to go
To meet the Iraqi foe

Was democracy the true goal
Or changing the Muslim soul

WMD required our science
Killing civilians required our soul

THERE WERE NO WMD

Thousands of innocents died
Could science be justified

Friendly bombs or firing squads

Dead by a dictator or friendly bomb
Which will our conscience choose

Born to Surprises

My first surprise was being born. I awakened to find food and get over the shock. My mother gave me Life, the surprise, which should have prepared me for all the surprises I was to receive from women. I was not born with a surprise meter, yet some of my surprises would be 11 on a scale of 10. I was surprised by a stinging on my legs by a peach tree switch swung by my mother. I was surprised when Martha Ballard kicked me in the shins in the second grade. I was surprised when my older brother told me that it was because she was attracted to me. I was surprised to receive a blue bicycle in the back of the cotton wagon when my dad returned from the cotton gin. It came by mail to the local post office. It was a surprise from my sister. I was surprised when my fifth grade girlfriend gave me a copy of *Moby Dick* for Christmas.

Surprises kept coming from the women in my life, some good, some bad.

I was surprised when my fiancée wrote to tell me that she was marrying my college roommate. I was in the Navy trying to survive boot camp. A bad short-term surprise turned into a good surprise, but the timing was a real surprise. I was surprised at 24 with my first birthday party given by a group of nurses from Northwestern University.

Surprises have continued, like marriage, and the good part of that bad surprise was the birth of my children. Those unexpected happenings are continuing but it still surprises me when a woman reaches out and touches me. These are delightful surprises in this chaotic world.

Who Am I (Thinking)

Who am I
A rocket scientist
A cotton picker
A songwriter
A husband and father
A wayfaring stranger
A friend
A dreamer
An optimist
A survivor
A loser
A winner
A son
A brother
A farmer
A dish washer, a waiter, a cook
A softball pitcher, a football player, a golfer
A poet—maybe

Nature

The most joyful of nature

Presented to all seeing life

Windblown moisture in the air

Light shining through

Bent wavelengths

Brilliant colors abstract or shapes

Of Earth inhabitants and its life

Observed by the ultimate

Life evolving to reflect

Seeing things differently

As I grow older I see things differently. Things are my philosophy and view of happenings as well as ideas. It is as if a new light is shining but constantly changing brightness and color. This change adds and distracts from my serial of life. My years are now just drippings, no longer full-flowing streams. The triggers for full flow are not even recognizable, but hope is still intact.

The rights and wrongs do not pull the same response as both have waned in importance. Sometimes this mellowness does not fit my wants and desires. Some memory strings can be pulled with a word or a glance. Being aware of the change hopefully slows down my negative responses. A change in the view makes for more art in my life; even in my memories the pictures become paintings with more color and meaning. I no longer feel trapped into the rhythm of anyone else but now walk to my own beat.

The music is often sad like a requiem for life as it used to be. But I also hear the music and rhythms of hope. Hope has no longer many years to fill. It no longer has the big economic demands, but health and happiness are the big drivers.

Impossible

I cannot disconnect from

What I see

What I read

What I think
   I know

But more important
I cannot disconnect

From my birth
From my childhood

From my education

From my loves

From my victories
From my failures

I cannot disconnect
To be someone else

Why

Why does chicken taste better
When I am holding the bone

Why do songs sound better
When I am holding the guitar

Why does all scenery look better
When I am seeing it with you

Why does the rose smell sweeter
When it is attached to you

Why does feeling feel better
When I am touching you

Why is my life better
When I am with you

American Indians

Cowboys and Indians, what fun play
My friends and I played every day
A game of war we did not understand
We did not know it was for the Indian land
Our ancestors took across the USA
It was their land the Indians had no say
Some fought back as we took their land
Some with only bows in their hand
We called the red man a savage race
Our ancestors wanted to kill and erase
My friends and I had not yet learned
We were not even concerned
And we did not know of the genocide
We were playing a game not justified
We cowboys were on the wrong side
Should have been on the Indian's side

II. Love or Something Like It

C.S. Lewis identified four kinds of love in his life. I know there are two. I know of their wane and wax. Some of these poems are my feelings as I experience the waxing and waning of love or something like it.

Dried Dreams

How do dreams dry
Is it like drying peaches
In the sun
On a tin roof
With the sweet juice
Evaporating to the sky
Going sun-seeking

Dream drying
Leaves a shell
Waiting to be reconstituted
Would you do that for me

A Pair

I thought

We

Were a pair

To keep

How was I to know

That you thought

We

Were a pair to throw away

You found

A better pairing

And

I

Was found

In

The

Discards

Beauty or Fashion

Torn jeans

Tattooed arms

The young lady

Wears and shows

At the beauty salon

Is it for beauty

Or just fashion

A New Day

What would a new day bring
When I was 2
My sister was born in the spring
I did not know
That it was the beginning
Of a lifetime of love
What would a new day carry
When my wife and I
Chose to marry
I did not know
That it was the beginning
Of a lifetime of love
What would a new day generate
When two sons
We would create
I did not know
That it was the beginning
Of a lifetime of love
What would happen one day in time
When my sister died too early at 39
I did not know
That it was the beginning

Of the rest of my life missing her
What would each new day convey
When other family members died
As I turned to face each after death day
I did not know that each loss would alter
My consciousness and my being

Natural Art

Your art weighs heavily
within me, like a painting
etched in stone, but
chiseled from flesh and bone
into eternity for
me to see. You were not
a copy but an
art form known only
to me. Surrendering to
your art is like diving
off a cliff and floating never
quite completing the dive.
Held up by your beauty
and intrigue of the creation
painted of you by you.
Intentional creation or
fortuitous it matters not
for I am drawn to the art
nature painted for me.

Pretty

Pretty is
As
Pretty does
Advice from my sister whom I loved.
Was this a comment on my girlfriend
Or her philosophy about women and men
I did not ask her before she died.
Keeping me straight she always tried.
I see pretty women throughout our land
But not much kindness do I see firsthand
A pretty woman without a smile
Not one to walk with down the aisle
But all women get pretty with kind acts
My sister really knew her facts
Pretty is
As
Pretty does
A way to find someone to love

Words

Your words
Gave me new thoughts

Your beauty
Gave me new feelings

Thoughts and feelings
A lifetime of enchantment

Waking

My mind
Wakes thinking of you
Standing in the moonlight
Casting a moon shadow
But more real than the days
Love light

Buttons

Buttons on blouses and shirts
I am better at unbuttoning
Than buttoning
Seems I change fingers for all thumbs
When buttoning
But fingers become agile
When unbuttoning—blouses
Could be related to a desire
For success

A Part of Me

Love is a part of me
Survives in my subconscious
Comes forth when expected
But also arrives unexpectedly
When the longings surface
At the sight of you

Message Mistakes

I had read you wrong
So many times
    1. The enticing smile

Not for me?
    2. Your conversation

Practice for after awhile
    3. The double entendre

Did not know the phrase was folded
    4. The song you sang

Was it for another's ears?
    5. The note you left upon my desk

Without an addressee
    6. Your dressing invitation with shoulders bare

Was it global?

    7. I even mistook your exit

For an entrance

    8. I thought our dance close to the beat

Was just a dance

All of these messages I misread until
You whispered
I love you

A Selfie

She sent herself through the air
Only a photograph sent to me
She was a maiden young and fair

Why would she even dare
She was a winner I could see
She sent herself through the air

Did she really think I could care
I had never seen her likes before
She was a maiden young and fair

Did she want to enter my lair
How did she know who I was
She sent herself through the air

Making me hope that I could snare
Or at least have a conversation
She was a maiden young and fair

Where were selfies when I was young
Life would have been a lot more fun
She sent herself through the air
She was a maiden young and fair

Curds and Whey

Clabber, not a very enticing word
When milk turns to the absurd
Like a relationship turned sour
Curdled into clabber in one fitful hour

When you called me to say good-bye
On your front porch sourness occurred
Where we had kissed often out of sight
And held each other long and tight

Love clobbered into clabber
Solid pieces floating in the whey
Forever separated on that day
When you chose to go away

The freshness of the love milk
Turned to a separated morose mass
Now memories have that sour taste
Remembering young love turned to waste

III. Happenings and Descriptions

These poems tell stories of happenings and also of the things I see. Happenings are difficult to pin down since we all see things differently. We certainly describe everything differently. It is almost as if Einstein's Theory of Relativity is at work in the cognitive process. Things can happen at the same time and yet can be viewed as if they were a light year apart by any two beings. Being different but similar keeps us communicating. Our previous experience with words fix our old and new descriptions. I hope I have provided some words to simulate your memories of happenings.

Fliver

A fliver was a car with fenders
Running boards and a rumble seat
To drive and sit in one
Was quite a treat
Front headlights were
Fender mounted
Tail lights stuck out behind
Running boards abounded
Below the doors
Were steps for getting
Onto a front or back seat
The rumble seat required
A more physical stretch
Stepping high upon
A fender before sliding
Into the seat
A great time in automobile
History for man
When his machine
Was a courting instrument
A fliver was once supreme

Haikus for May 2017

The new jeans were torn
The knees before being worn
Now it is fashion

When I was a lad
Wearing patches was the fad
When the knees wore out

Sometimes on our knees
We prayed for a soothing breeze
To come down the rows

We would wear old jeans
New pairs were beyond our means
Patches were the fad

Knees became threadbare
And patches were sewn with care
That was the fashion

Farmer, Ship Builder and Soldier

He left the farm
To build ships
Then he served in the army
Penned in a foxhole
On the island of Okinawa
He survived shrapnel
Loneliness when his buddy
Jumped and ran
His body pierced
With machine gun bullets
From the Japanese on higher ground
My dad stayed in the foxhole
Without food and water
He survived even the triage
Allocated for those dying
He fought for freedom yours and mine
And for a land
A piece of which he never owned

Getting By

Dry land farming was a losing game
Even when the spring rains came
My dad went through lots of dry
Always getting on with getting by
Plants and animals his livelihood
Their need for water was understood
Both had to give an extra try
If the farm family was to get by
Dad believed in free enterprise
Before farms got up to profit size
Not much profit in just getting by
But every year was another try

Impact

Don't drag the handle through impact
Extend your arms when you take it back
Bring the handle down pointing to the green
The club head lags but should be seen
Redundancy keep your eye on the ball
Swinging too hard might produce a fall
Avoid hitting from behind the ball
Follow through and finish tall
Dragging that handle in front of impact
Will reduce club head speed, it's a fact

Current events

The news, more rain for today
Pages about grown men who play
Baseball is coming to a close
News about Cowboys and their foes
About games to be performed
And what QB will be stormed
News about coming elections
Should be in the back sections
Ideology wars are being fought
Perhaps they are all for naught

I read my news in black and white
While others hold their i-pads light
I haven't placed an i-pad on trial
Holding a newspaper is more my style
I drink my coffee with my news
While reading other points of view
I shall continue in my reading fashion
A folded newspaper is my passion

Happenings

It was a happening, not a catastrophe
When I hit the golf ball in the pond
It was not like she said good-bye to me
But of that new Titlist I was really fond

It was a happening, not a catastrophe
When I dropped the egg upon the floor
I had no one to blame for it but me
I blamed old age as I went out the door

It was a happening, not a catastrophe
When I removed the price tag with scissors
Leaving holes where threads used to be
Things like this happen to old geezers

It was a happening, not a catastrophe
When I didn't score and we lost the game
No one put the blame on me
But it was a loss just the same

It was a happening, not a catastrophe
When from the great height I fell
I should not have been in the tree
But it made a story for me to tell

It was a happening, not a catastrophe
When I tried to write this and failed
It was to be a poem as you can see
That was before my muse had sailed

Animal Companions

A farm boy's early companions are
Dogs who play and roosters who chase
Love from one and hate from the other
Until my sister was born when I was
Two years and three months old
My dogs Blackie and Bolger
Were my playmates and protectors

The non-playmate was
A white, red comb, leghorn rooster
Who chased me every time
I stepped off the back porch alone
I cannot tell you why the dogs
Liked me
I cannot tell you why the white rooster
Hated me
My dog companions were always
In the protective mode
The white leghorn was always in
The attack mode

The leghorn history was short

The dogs lived through

Attacking a wolf pack

With my dad's help

With a needle

He sewed up both their bellies

With thread from the treadle sewing machine

They both lived until I was seven

Attached Light

We sat on a bench
Legs under the oil cloth covered table
The flame attached to a wick soaked with
Coal oil from the lamp
Attached its light to the pages
Of our schoolbooks
We also ate our suppers
With this attached light
The flame always flickered
When the breeze came through
The open door
We were free to read
By that coal oil light
Before we went to bed
The end of the evening came
When the flame was unattached
By blowing into the globe
You had to have a straight mouth
And a forceful blow
To unattach the flame from the wick
Still soaked with the coal oil

The Sisyphean Game

Golf is a Sisyphean game
Each day its players just the same
They start with tee and a ball
Some swing fast others stall
It is such Sisyphean repetition
Getting the ball into position
To roll once more into the hole
For fewer strokes souls are sold
We do not know the god's name
Who first presented the golf game
But it must be a god's punishment
Keeping us golfers so diligent
For just like the travails of Sisyphus
Hitting the ball every day is ridiculous

It is even incredulous
And often humorous

Jungle Animal

She was a jungle animal
Always swinging on a tree
Thinking she would not fall
She knew the geography
Trees she knew best of all
Where she learned to flirt
Learning had only taken one fall
Now she was a tree expert
She knew how to attract
Even the dullest of men
Even Tarzan would react
She was no mannequin
A queen among all the rest
Living life "swinging" happily
In her world she was the best
The picture of jungle aristocracy

About the Poet

Hollis Davis has a bachelor's degree in chemistry from Texas Tech University and an MBA from TCU. He is retired from the aerospace industry. His professional work was in composite materials for rocket motors, one of the 33 activities for making money from childhood to retirement. Writing poetry is number 34. This is his sixth book of poetry. He also has a book of memoirs entitled, *Rungs of the Ladder*, published in 2010.

Mr. Davis has recently started helping teach English. He plays golf and has shot his age, 87. He also enjoys fishing for bass with his son, Barry, a mechanical engineer who works in the aerospace industry. His other son, Dr. C.B. Davis, is a history and drama teacher. His daughter, Vickie, has worked in hospice care for many years.

He started guitar lessons over ten years ago and goes with a singing group, which includes his wife Pansy, to Memory Care Assisted Living each month. He has written several songs. One he wrote for his uncle is entitled, "How Long Do I Have to Live to Be an Old Man?" It is available on CDBaby.

About Path Publishing

Path Publishing began in 1993 and has published a variety of uplifting books and other projects over the years. We tend to specialize in general and Christian nonfiction, poetry, biographies, and self-help. Our website, PathPublishing.com, contains the works of many writers. In the past we have been listed in these publications: *Christian Writers' Market Guide*, *The Directory of Little Magazines and Small Presses*, and *The Writer*.

To order a paperback copy of *Common and Uncommon Thoughts*, purchase at Amazon.com/books. You can also send $11.99 plus $3.50 shipping for a total of $15.49 (Texans add 8.25 percent sales tax for a total of $16.77) to Path Publishing, 4302 SW 51st #121, Amarillo, Texas 79109-6159.

www.ingramcontent.com/pod-product-compliance
Lightning Source LLC
Chambersburg PA
CBHW071640040426
42452CB00009B/1711